I0408481

THE PATH TO BECOMING A SUCCESSFUL LIFE COACH

PHILLIP ELLENBURG AND MARCIA HAYES

THE GOOD LIFE
ELLENBURG EDUCATIONAL SERIES

CHAPTERS

The Good Life
ELLENBURG EDUCATIONAL SERIES

THE PATH TO BECOMING A SUCCESSFUL LIFE COACH

INTRODUCTION

THE ROLE OF A LIFE COACH

A life coach is able to give a client a true picture of exactly where they are today in all facets of their life, the areas they want to change and a realistic road map to achieve those changes. A life coach educates, assists and guides the client to achieve maximum results in performance and reaching obtainable goals.

THE REALITY

Life coaching can be the most rewarding job you will ever have. When you see a client reach a goal, there is an intrinsic value that few other jobs can offer. Life coaching is unique way to make a living and it can be very profitable (or <u>not</u>). Most of your success will be based on your marketing ability. The goal of any job is to make money but do not think coaching is easy work. You need to think through the following issues which will be addressed in separate chapters and decide whether or not you are willing to commit yourself to the time and expense of starting a new business.

Do you have the skill set necessary to be a coach?

Are you ready to commit to the time, effort and expense of starting a new business?

Can you support yourself while you are building a business and can you make a living at coaching?

You will need to write a business plan and possibly get a loan. You will have to constantly market yourself and your business. You will have to have a professional website. You will have to be flexible in selecting how, where and to whom you will offer your services.

You will also need to identify and develop what works best for you in the actual process and planning of your work. A copy of our process is included within this book and we have been very successful with this approach. You are welcome to use all or any part of this plan while you are building your own.

You will also want to consider the potential liabilities you may encounter which means you not only have to know your boundaries but you also must know the laws of your state for starting a business and your state and federal tax responsibilities.

Finally, if you are still determined that this is right for you after all of the considerations, you are well on your way to becoming a successful coach!

CHAPTER I

DO YOU HAVE THE SKILL SET NECESSARY TO BE A COACH?

Do you have the skill set necessary to be a coach?

People often think about coaching because there are no set requirements (yet) to hold one's self out as a coach. There are several places you can get "certified" on line but it is not necessary and these certifications can be costly and carry little weight. So, the real question here is can you be an effective coach?

The answer to this question depends solely on what you bring to the table. Just having a desire to "help" someone is not enough You need to have insight, foresight, tenacity, ethics, and organizational and life skills. Most of all, you need to be able to convey these things to your client.

Many of us have educations and have worked in the business for some time. We also have references. Starting new, you have to be able to sell yourself over someone else who seemingly has more to give. This is not as daunting as it looks. People who are going to put down good money for a service are going to shop around for who they think will give them what they want and need. Remember, everyone has to start somewhere and you need to have a solid website and then present with a confidence, and enthusiasm that makes you a more viable candidate.

Life coaching has had a bad reputation primarily because even a few years ago people did not understand the concept. While it has gained a lot of acceptance since then, it is our responsibility to project respect for this profession and that means you not only represent yourself but you also represent the entire field. This is one of the reasons we tell coaches in our classes not to discount their services. There are actually few people in the general population who can be an effective life coach because of the skill set necessary. The people who have what it takes and decide to be life coaches need to be compensated accordingly even if they are new to the profession.

CHAPTER II

WHAT YOU CAN EXPECT WHEN STARTING A NEW BUSINESS

What can you expect when starting a new business? It is going to take time, money, a commitment and it would help to have a sense of humor.

Remember that you want to be a life coach for a reason and hold on to that when you get tired and you will get tired. When people start their own business they often work unreasonably long hours because they are vested in its success. Starting any business is risky, particularly in a relatively new field and one where the "soft sciences" are involved. Also, you do not yet have your own formula for how you want to run the business and you will, undoubtedly, have to invest more money than you initially budgeted.

However, the positives of starting your own business are immeasurable. You will be following your passion, you can be creative, you will be helping people achieve their goals and you can be your own boss. It might be advantageous to write a list of positives and negatives and post them where you can re-visit and tweak them from time to time.

CHAPTER III

CAN YOU MAKE A LIVING AT COACHING?

Can you make a living at coaching? Absolutely. You are offering a fantastic service. Think of it in these terms. What would a person be willing to pay to make significant life changes and/or have a better quality of life? Coaching someone to another level towards self-actualization is immeasurable in a dollar sense. People considering coaching understand this and are willing to pay for the service.

You are going to encounter people with all kinds of different agendas. As an example, we have actually coached people from all different social strata's. We have had several people who came for one session because they wanted to know how to be a life coach and this prompted our classes and our books. You will also see people with unrealistic expectations or people you cannot or should not help. Do not be afraid to pass by a client who is not serious or who is going to drain you.

You have got to decide how and how much you want to bill for your services. It is beneficial to put this on your website but others disagree. It has always been our philosophy that we charge "x" amount of dollars per session regardless of your income. Putting the amount of each service and breaking down the services on the website allow us to avoid negotiation and we would rather concentrate on content. Others coaches prefer to charge for what they think the cost of their time for that particular client will be and still, others like to use a sliding scale.

Just starting a new business, do your research. Go to different websites and see what they are charging and compare your services to theirs. You are not going to get rich overnight but you do have the potential to earn a substantial income. Is every life coach successful? No. But with hard work, good marketing and even maybe some luck, you can be. If you don't believe you can be successful, you have the wrong mindset to be a coach.

CHAPTER IV

YOU NEED A BUSINESS PLAN

You will have to write a business plan. You absolutely have to have a business plan. You cannot get a loan without a business plan and even if you don't need a loan, you do need to know what you are doing.

A good business plan will define what you are doing, how you are going to do it, where you are going, how long you think it will take you to get there and it will keep you on track with money. Your plan needs to include a budget and it will allow you to see where your money is going.

A good business plan is also a great marketing tool. Take advantage of the Small Business Administration and online resources to project how successful you are and whether or not you have hit the right markets. You can, and probably will, revise your business plan several times to reflect your situation. Not everything will follow your projections so do not be afraid to be flexible and creative.

There are several places you can get a free business plan online and you just add your information. You will be going back to this plan over and over again. It will hold you accountable and you keep you from making some costly mistakes.

Also, do your homework. Always be on top of what is happening in your business and the plan will do that for you. You may be a great coach but if you are not crunching the numbers, you might not be as successful financially as you need to be.

CHAPTER V

CHOOSE YOUR AUDIENCE

You need to decide which population(s) you are willing and able to accommodate. Life coaches take on many roles and you want to coach where you are most comfortable and where you believe you would be most effective.

You are not restricted to one-on-one coaching.

Classes and seminars can be very lucrative and they almost always generate new business.

You may also want to explore business coaching. It pays well and usually requires only one or two days on the premises. This is a great perk for an employer to offer his employees and many businesses do offer this benefit. You can work with some employee assistance programs and even offer in-services for employee relations. Progressive businesses offer wellness programs that often include business/life coaches.

Also, the religious community is starting to grasp the benefit of having life coaches take some of the burden off of over-worked pastors.

The legal system has started using coaches particularly when it comes to youth. Government has long known that basic skills workers and psycho-social workers have made a difference in behaviors and the system is now starting to incorporate life coaches.

The need for life coaches in the teens is a wide open area particularly when it comes to sexual identity issues   We know the suicide rate for kids with specific issues is very, very high.

There is no end to the possibilities of the populations you could serve. You must decide where your passion is and target that group(s). Your business plan will keep you on track so if the market you have chosen is not productive, you can re-visit and re-evaluate your plan.

Ultimately, you will have to choose the population(s) that you market and are "willing and able" to accommodate.

CHAPTER VI

YOU NEED A WEBSITE

You must have a domain and a viable website. There are many resources on line with templates and you could go from there. However, this is no place to skimp and you may even consider having a professional do this for you.

We know in real estate curb appeal is important. It is no different here. People are going to subliminally get messages from how your website looks. They are going to notice your syntax, your graphics, your organizational and even your grammatical skills. It has to be easy to read and maneuver. These things are as important as the content.

Content is important. You need to have clarity and you need to be precise. No one wants to search for your message or your services. According to numerous studies, people only read 20% of what they see and while we cannot verify that is true, you can be assured that first impressions and a clear message will keep them interested. Conversely, most people will not continue to read something that is boring or difficult to understand.

Make certain you have contact information because it is easier to get someone to take advantage of your services if you get to speak with them. Don't be afraid to give out information. Even if you told someone exactly how you do everything, they do not have your intellectual gifts and know-how so they cannot replicate your services.

Don't forget to put the website in the budget.

CHAPTER VII

MARKET, MARKET, MARKET

You have to MARKET, MARKET, MARKET. Marketing can absolutely make you or break you. If you are not good at marketing, hire someone or enlist a friend or family member because you need to get your services known or you will not make any money.

Moreover, marketing is an animal all its own. There is so much to know that there are hundreds of books on the subject. So just starting, keep it as simple but as extensive as possible.

You have to have a business card, you need to visit places that will generate business, look up all the pertinent meetings and attend them, make yourself known in the community and be willing to put your cards everywhere.

There are a plethora of internet marketing tools. Your website will drive business by key words and there are several other social media sites where you can market.

Advertising on television is very expensive so probably not a viable option. However, consider a blurb on the radio. While radio stations will offer you many different contracts, don't get suckered in. The truth is you can offer to be a guest on one or several of their segments including maybe even a once-a-week call in. Also local television stations and even the local news often have local small businesses come in and introduce themselves.

Consider a pod cast. This allows you to cover a large population. This gives you your own show with your own followers.

Newspapers are always an option and you can get some reasonable rates (even free) if you negotiate but again, choose the newspapers that target your population which probably isn't the daily newspaper.

Create your own marketing network and saturate as many markets as you can. Give out business cards and follow up. Make contacts and keep records. Referrals can be a significant share of your business.

Finally, you can always get a books on marketing , search the internet and do it your way. Just a word of caution. Advertising can absolutely deplete your budget so keep a close eye on your business plan and remember that once you are established, this part of your budget should be minimal.

Put it in the budget.

.

CHAPTER VIII

COMMUNICATION

Your communication skills are going to set you apart from everyone else. Work on your weak points and emphasize your strengths. You have to decide what kind of median you want to commit to in order to communicate effectively with your client.

You can, of course, use the internet and while that is a feasible option, it can be impersonal. If you have a client that is not in your immediate area, you may want to consider going to their area and proceed with a concentrated coaching.

You are going to need an address and phone dedicated to your business. You will probably want office space especially if you plan on the majority of your business being local. You need to figure this in the budget. It is possible to get virtual office space but, either way, it is an expense.

CHAPTER IX

INITIAL QUESTIONNAIRE FOR CLIENT

All of your creativity really begins from here and through the following chapters.   Ideally you want to obtain as much information about your client as possible so that you can metaphorically walk in his/her shoes and thus begin the work.

A questionnaire is a **GREAT** way to do this. The answers to the questions you ask can be very telling and will enable you to produce a good picture of the "present" client. Once that picture is translated to a graphic for us (you can choose any format you want), both you and the client have a realistic starting point.

A questionnaire will also help you identify the clients you do not or should not take. You will want to put a lot of time and thought into your questions and as much time into the answers. For example, our questionnaire is 50 questions. We ask things like, are you taking any medications, are you aware of any mental health issues, do you use recreational drugs and do you have a therapist. Medications can tell us about potential physical conditions, mental health issues need to be directed to a therapist, recreational drugs speak to an avoidance and possibly and addiction and if the client has a therapist, you want a release of information so you can talk to the therapist and hopefully work in tandem with her to ensure the best possible results for your client.

We like to email the questionnaire to the client and have him email it back before the first meeting. However, it can be just as effective to have the questions ready and spend your initial meeting asking the questions. This will give you an extra session and depending how you want to structure your plan, this may work even better for you. We have never had any objection to any of our questionnaires. However, I want to emphasize that while life coaches are not under the same HIPPA laws as health care professionals, it is still important to maintain your ethical responsibilities. At Ellenburg Educational Systems we consistently emphasize to our clients (and state on the questionnaires) that all work is strictly confidential. In fact, all clients at Ellenburg are assigned a number so that if their situation is discussed anywhere, only the client's number is given with no name. This ensures the client's identity even within our organization. Further, our coaches are carefully chosen for not only their education and credentials but also their ability to be non-judgmental, life-affirming and dedicated to the growth and privacy of the people they serve.

If you are working with a business, the questions will be different but the objective to accumulate vital information is still the same. Life coaches are not utilized to evaluate or change a business. However, they are more specifically asked to address a mind set or specific challenges within the system. For example, a coach may be asked to give a sensitivity seminar to managers. When working within confines such as a business, it is very important to understand the rules, not over-step your boundaries and foster a lasting relationship with the Human Resource department. (This also gives you an advantage when you propose that you stay on site for one or two days a week to address questions from employees to ensure that they maintain a sense of wellness). Also, a coach can be of great assistance in directing people to community resources. A coach can be make a very good living at just working for a company for just a day or two a week. A cost/benefit analysis often convinces a company to hire a life-coach as a great perk for the employees. Everyone wins.

CHAPTER X

THE PROCESS

The actual process of structuring a program has a lot to do with expectations. What does your client actually want to accomplish. Often, after putting up a graphic of where your client presently "lives", he finds that the original objective is not what he really wants to accomplish but something entirely different.

It is important to be astute, observant and aware when dealing with your client. You must never, never put yourself in a compromising position that could be interpreted as therapy. When together you have identified the goal then you need to show your client a clear path to reaching that objective. For example, let us say a client comes to you to lose weight. You are certainly capable of exploring different diet options with him. You are within your scope of practice to help him make meal choices and holding him accountable for and understanding that he has a right to make choices but those choices not included in the original diet plan will delay his weight loss. You can motivate your client and how you do that is up to you. Some examples are constantly revisiting the program and continuing to make it fit your client's lifestyle, motivational quotes, lots of pep talks, having him keep a journal, calling, meeting him for a meal, etc. etc. The more creative and inspirational you can be, the better coach you are. However, you are not trained to go into the psychological reasons he may have made for making those choices. That would be a therapist. It is essential that you know the difference between a life coach and a therapist.

You also need to be acutely aware of you client's needs. If he is asking for achievement on something you cannot or are not willing to work on, you need to say so and direct him to a different resource. A good example of this is addiction. This should not be in your scope of practice unless you are a certified or licensed drug counselor. People can have seizures and die in withdrawal. Just because you think you can does not mean you should. You are not a trained health care professional. Make a list of local resources and be able to direct people to the appropriate places. Give people the opportunity to access a wide range of professionals.

Always remember that you absolutely must be factual without being judgmental. This is about your client, not you. Shaming someone NEVER works. Conversely, neither are you his best friend. A great coach is always inspiring a client, acknowledging achievements and milestones and making strength out of weakness. However, you must always maintain your professional position. You can count on being tested but never make an exception.

You also need to be acutely aware of your client's needs. If he is asking for a goal that is beyond your scope, is unethical or something you cannot or are not willing to work on, you need to say so and direct him to a different resource. An example of this is a person who wants to stop intrusive thoughts on child porn. This should not be in your scope of practice and you do not have the proper tools to take on such a request. Money is always tempting particularly when you first start out but you have to be honest, fair and practical. Just because you think you can handle a difficult situation does not always mean you should. You are not trained to be a health care professional regardless of how competent you may feel in a particular area.

Another test some coaches face is their opinion versus their client's position. Remember that this is your client's life and his choices may not be your choices. But they ARE his choices. If you try to direct him in a different way, you are asking him to live your values and opinions. If your client's choices get him to where he wants to go, you have to be able to affirm his desire to proceed his way and be totally on board. If you are unable to do this, it will be an unhealthy relationship and you need to terminate your agreement so you do not interfere with your client's progress.

CHAPTER XI

THE BLUEPRINT

The program. Regardless of the reason a client has decided to use our services, we give everyone an overall picture of where they are at. We get the information from our questionnaire and two of the questions are: "What are the most important six things in your life?" and "How much of your time is spent in each area?". Again we do a pie chart showing where the client is now and an arrow to a second pie chart showing where he would ideally like to be in these areas. This is a very telling method for your client to actually see his quality of life right at the moment.

Then we talk with the client and ask what he has decided he wants to work on. It may be a particular issue, or it may be one of the six areas he has identified in the questionnaire. Once that has been established, we build our plan from there.

Get a clear-cut detailed plan of how to get from A-Z and start immediately. You will have to use your own creativity in conjunction with your client's thinking and set small goals. Educate, inspire, and motivate, motivate, motivate.

How you set about motivating your client and keeping him on track is something that will be uniquely determined by you. You have lots of tools in addition to creativity. It will be necessary to implement many tools including having a client keep a journal.

You will have to have designated times to meet and also determine how accessible you want to be on phone, text, computer. Stick your meeting times. It is a "show up and suit up" principle. This gives you legitimacy and it gives your client accountability. Of course, you need to be flexible, but meeting times should be mostly stable as it shows the seriousness and commitment of both parties.

You will have to determine how much time you are going to give each client and what your fees will be. It is our practice to give each client six (6) weeks. It is our philosophy that the client should be well along on their goals by that time. If they are not, one of you has not done your job. In which case, the business relationship has failed and it should be re-evaluated and the client should probably be referred to a different professional.

We meet with a client once a week at the same time and often see them several times between their designated times, depending on their needs and their progress. You have to think way out of the box on how you are going to encourage and support your client. For example, you may find yourself showing up at an event to reinforce your client's ability to give a speech, etc.

It is also our standard to be available by text always although our clients understand that if we receive a text we will answer it within 6 hours but we usually answer it right away. We are not as generous with the phone as we are busy and we will not take a call when we are with a client. So we have unlimited phone calls between 9-5 with a 2 hour turn around. We generally do not take phone calls at night and that is a boundary that only an emergency will supersede. .

Fees vary. Because we are established, we usually use a set fee which includes everything including follow-up for a month. You will want to look at lots of websites to determine what you think is an ideal rate. You can set a fee that is all inclusive or you can structure your fee in any way that works for you depending on the circumstances. Also, you need to determine how and when you want to get paid. Be crystal clear here so you do not find yourself working for free. We like 50% up front, another 25% on three and the last 25% on week five. Some clients like to pay by the week as it is easiest for them. We generally that 50% up front because we do the majority of paperwork in the beginning of the program and it also shows a commitment on the client's part.

Take into consideration that even after your contract with your client is done, you will want to follow-up.

CHAPTER XII

CLIENTS YOU SHOULD NOT TAKE

Clients you should not take. This is so important. **YOUR ARE NOT A MENTAL HEALTH PROFESSIONAL**. Life coaching is not health care. Coaching belongs in the educational field and it is your job to mentor your clients, not treat them physically or emotionally. These two professions are totally different and your coaching must never cross over into the mental health field.

Until you get more seasoned, you will probably want to accept everyone. First, you don't want to do any harm and second, you don't want to get sued which is a very real possibility. You might decide to buy professional liability insurance and this depends on a lot of factors including how you structure your business.

You should not take people who are suffering from addictions and want to detox or are detoxing. ALL addictions require mental health professionals. Again, life coaching is NEVER therapy.

You should not accommodate people who have unrealistic goals or think you will do their work for them.

You should not take people who believe are insincere or who present with a capacity to hurt you in any way.

You need to consider whether or not you want to work with someone who has a health issue that is not being addressed.

You should not take people who want a guarantee.

Finally, if you have any uneasiness with a client for any reason at all, refer them out. There are many people who would benefit from your services. You do not have to take anyone who you think is going to be problematic in any way.

After you have decided to work with someone, do not be afraid to terminate a contract when you sense something is wrong. In fact, this should be part of your agreement up front with your client. Either party can end the relationship at any time. Better to lose some money than to lose a lot of money or get a bad reputation.

CHAPTER XIII

LEGAL RESPONSIBILITY

Legal Responsibility. It is your responsibility to understand the laws of your state for licensing and starting a new business. You will have to decide whether you want to have a d/b/a, a partnership, an LLP or a corporation. You may need some help with this. It will be easy to understand the differences but much more difficult to understand the tax consequences of each. The best thing to do is to consult with an accountant. Most of them are very generous and give you a first meeting free. This sends a good message and means you will probably use them again when you need a service.

Because you will be getting money, it can be tempting to use cash on something right away. Go back to your business plan first. You need to ensure that you are staying in line with your financial needs and goals and part of this is what you need to set aside for taxes.

Remember that, legally, taxes are due as soon as the money is earned..

When you get money, you also need to evaluate how much money you are making vs what you need and project out a year to see if you are in line with a financially sound business venture.

CHAPTER XIV

NOW IT IS ALL ABOUT YOU

Now, it is all about you. We have sketched out a viable path for success in this book. You need to fill in the creativity part. You have unlimited power to make yourself a success.

Stay motivated. When you need to hash things out or need some motivation, have a designated "go to" person and use him.

Reach out to others in the field. We pride ourselves in what we do and how we do it. We try to be generous to others in the field and we hope everyone shares this philosophy.

Believe in yourself, your motivations, and your ability to help others.

YOU'VE GOT THIS!

www.ingramcontent.com/pod-product-compliance
Lightning Source LLC
Chambersburg PA
CBHW071258280526
45788CB00004B/1767